SMILE

D1113359

SMILE

SELL MORE

with
Amazing Customer Service

KIRT MANECKE

**SOLID
PRESS**
LLC

Made in the U.S.A.

Copyright © 2013 by Kirt Manecke

All rights reserved.

This publication is protected under the U.S. Copyright Act of 1976 and all other applicable international, federal, state, and local laws. No part of this publication may be reproduced or transmitted in any form or by any means, mechanical or electronic, including photocopying and recording, or by any information storage and retrieval system, without permission in writing from the publisher, except in the case of brief excerpts in reviews and articles.

Published by Solid Press, LLC. Inquiries about this book should be addressed to the publisher: Solid Press, LLC, PO Box 145, Milford, MI 48381, or kirt@smilethebook.com.

Library of Congress Control Number: 2012911797

www.SmiletheBook.com

LEGAL NOTICE
Please note that much of this publication is based on personal experience that has worked for the author. You should use this information as you see fit and at your own risk. Your particular situation may not be exactly the same, and you should adjust your use of the information accordingly. Use your own best judgment in all situations. Nothing in this book is meant to replace legal/professional advice.

Special discounts for bulk purchases are available to your company, nonprofit, educational institution, professional association, or other organization for educational or training purposes, reselling, subscription or other incentives, sales promotions, employee premiums, corporate gifts, or fundraising. For details, please contact the Special Sales Department, Solid Press, LLC, PO Box 145, Milford, MI 48381, or kirt@smilethebook.com.

Summary: A quick, easy-to-read customer service and sales guidebook to help employers and employees delight customers and dramatically increase sales.

Book Design: Rae Ann Spitzenberger

ISBN 978-0-9850762-3-8

A portion of the proceeds from the sale of this book are donated to animal welfare.

*To my uncle Gene, who taught me
how to sell — and how to live.*

---

*And to my parents, John and Betsy,
who have always been there for me.*

CONTENTS

CHAPTER ONE
THE TOP TEN
HOW TO MAKE YOUR CUSTOMERS SMILE (AND BUY!) . . 11

CHAPTER TWO
KEEP THEM SMILING
MORE TOP CUSTOMER SERVICE TECHNIQUES 31

CHAPTER THREE
SELL MORE
MORE SECRETS TO SUCCESSFUL SELLING 49

CHAPTER FOUR
WHEN THERE'S A PROBLEM
TURNING PROBLEMS INTO SUCCESS STORIES 75

CHAPTER FIVE
CREATE A CUSTOMER FOR LIFE

ACKNOWLEDGEMENTS

Writing a book is a team effort — I doubt many people could go it alone. Thanks from the bottom of my heart to all those who have contributed to this project: Becky Ferguson, Ryan Ferguson, Gale Dettling, Rebecca Leite, Tom Montgomery, John Bongort, Joe Keller, Jennifer Foss, Karen Friesen, Robin Quinn, Karen McDiarmid, Hugh McDiarmid, Jr., Colleen Kilpatrick, Laurie Luketic, Ann Longanecker, Jordan Mercedes, Dave Csatari, Lisa Feist, Lindsay Cotter, Peter Wottowa, Rich Lindhorst, Dawn Weinfurtner, Bruce Montagne, Ted Owen, Maureen Perri, Ken Hiebel, April Slay, and the helpful trio of women at Main Street Art in downtown Milford, Michigan.

A special thank you to my parents, John and Betsy Manecke, and to my late uncle Gene Balogh, whose spirit and work have always been an inspiration to me.

Thank you to my wonderful editor Jean Borger for pulling this book together.

And finally, thank you to all my friends and colleagues, including those not mentioned here, for their very valuable insight, patience, and support in this endeavor.

INTRODUCTION

When we give, we receive — when a business does something good for somebody, that somebody feels good about them.
BEN COHEN, BEN & JERRY'S ICE CREAM

The Delightful Deli

This book is based on the simple premise that **good service is good business** — that if you treat your customers right, you'll be rewarded in return. Doing what customers love is a proven, guaranteed way to increase customer loyalty and sell more, without gimmicks or expensive marketing.

When I think about amazing customer service — the kind that dazzles people and makes them want to tell their friends — I think of Zingerman's Deli in Ann Arbor, Michigan. Zingerman's is an Ann Arbor institution beloved by locals and out-of-towners alike. The deli welcomes over 500,000 visitors a year and boasts sales of more than $12 million annually, due in no small part to a culture of exceptional customer service.

On a recent visit to Zingerman's I felt like I'd landed in a food lover's version of Disney World. My friend and I were greeted by an employee the second we walked in the door.

His "Hello!" was warm and enthusiastic, he made great eye contact, and his smile was genuine.

In the 20 minutes we spent exploring the deli before sitting down to eat our sandwiches, we interacted with at least five different employees — all of them smiling, welcoming, seeming to anticipate our every desire. They asked us where we were from, answered questions, recommended their favorite foods, and offered samples of anything in the store. We found ourselves smiling as we walked out the door.

Zingerman's always seems to be full of paying customers — even at 3 p.m. on a weekday — and it's no wonder. Great customer service makes customers smile. Smiling customers spend more money, become profitable repeat customers, and tell their friends. It really is a guaranteed recipe for success.

With the advent of social media, the marketing power of satisfied customers has only increased. Sixty-two percent of consumers have used social media for customer service issues, and these consumers will typically tell over 40 potential customers about exceptional customer service. This is amazing news for anyone reading this book!

But beware — dissatisfied customers pack even more power. Consumers who use social media for customer service issues will typically tell over 50 potential customers about poor service. And overall, one in four consumers will post a negative comment on a social media site following a poor customer service experience.

When you factor in the ripple effect of social media, one negative testimonial can easily reach hundreds, if not thousands, of potential customers. No business or salesperson can afford this type of negative advertising, but many are getting it without even knowing.

A Kid and His Punching Bag

On the flip side, an unhappy customer can be an opportunity in disguise. When I was 10 years old, I had a punching bag that leaked. I decided to send it back and wrote a letter to Everlast explaining my problem. I really didn't expect to hear anything back, but two weeks later a package arrived. To my surprise and delight, it contained a nice letter from Everlast — and a brand new punching bag.

The story might have ended there, but the new bag also leaked. I sent it back again, this time really expecting the cold shoulder. To my shock and amazement, Everlast sent me *another* nice letter along with *another* replacement punching bag — this time, their top of the line model. This bag did not leak, and I went on to use it happily for many years.

Needless to say, I was thrilled by my experience with Everlast (picture me as a boy smiling from ear to ear), and I've been a satisfied customer ever since. I am *still* telling my punching bag story, even after all these years. Everlast not only won me back with their amazing customer service, they created a customer, and an ambassador, for life.

It doesn't surprise me that, after more than 100 years in business, Everlast continues to be a brand leader. They truly know how to create satisfied customers and increase sales in the process. On average, a satisfied (but formerly frustrated) customer will tell five people about the great job a company did resolving their issue (not to mention people like me who tell far more). That's 25 positive reviews for

every five complaints handled well. And this positive advertising is absolutely free.

Resolving complaints effectively is just one way to make
your customers smile and create positive word of mouth
marketing. In this book, you'll learn dozens more. As you
use the simple yet powerful customer service and sales
techniques presented here, you'll watch as your customers
— or clients, patients, or donors — become loyal fans and
ambassadors.

Why This Book?

Too often customer satisfaction is ignored or taken for
granted. While 80% of companies *think* they're providing superior service, customers say only 8% are hitting the
mark. Nine in ten Americans say that businesses "fail to ex-
ceed" their expectations. Poor customer service costs U.S.
businesses an estimated $83 billion a year.

There are plenty of sales and customer service books out
there, and many of them are very good. The advantage this
book has over others is that it's a quick and easy read. This
means: 1) you'll actually read it, and 2) you can start today.
You can read this book cover to cover in 60 minutes or less
— or work chapter by chapter picking up a new technique
in just minutes a day.

Early in my career, I established, owned, and ran a highly
successful award-winning specialty store. Fundamental to
its success was a six-week employee training program that
I created to guarantee outstanding customer service, ensure
repeat business and positive word of mouth marketing, and
maximize sales.

The results were nothing short of amazing. Employees gained the confidence to interact with and satisfy customers, shoppers became buyers and ambassadors, and the store saw record sales.

In *Smile*, I've collected together powerful tips and techniques from this training program and from over 30 years of successful selling. These techniques will help you create an army of fans and ambassadors — customers who will stick by you, become customers for life, and spread the word about your business to others through testimonials and referrals.

IF YOU'RE AN EMPLOYER, THIS BOOK WILL HELP YOU:

- Increase sales, donations, repeat business, and positive buzz — starting today!
- Achieve record service numbers and profits
- Save money on expensive training
- Train and orient new employees
- Refresh and upgrade skills for seasoned staff
- Improve employee confidence, morale, and productivity

IF YOU'RE AN EMPLOYEE, THIS BOOK WILL HELP YOU:

- Build the service and sales skills you need to succeed in your job
- Energize and advance your career
- Become comfortable and confident with sales or fundraising
- Build life-long customer relationships
- Enjoy your work more than you ever imagined

Whether you're an employer or an employee, this simple, practical guide will help you make immediate, dramatic improvements to your customer service and sales — improvements that will help you increase customer satisfaction and sell more.

Who Should Read This Book

If you work with people on a regular basis — in person, on the phone, online, or via written correspondence, this book is for you. If you work in sales or fundraising, if you own or run a business or nonprofit or work for a government agency, if you regularly or periodically communicate with clients or customers, if you provide any type of service, dispense information, or resolve complaints — in all of these cases and more, this book is for you.

THIS BOOK IS PERFECT FOR:

- Sales, customer service, and other professionals looking to succeed and advance their careers
- Employers and managers seeking a powerful, cost-effective training resource to improve customer service and increase sales
- Young people entering the job market for the first time
- People switching jobs
- Nonprofit staff and volunteers
- Anyone who works with the public

Whatever your enterprise, you'll learn how easy it is to dazzle your customers and keep them coming back and talking positively about you and your business.

This book also includes sales tips to help you if you are one of the many employees who are uncomfortable with or afraid of selling (or fundraising) or who simply don't have a lot of experience or training in sales. The tips and techniques presented here will help you listen, ask the right questions, and sell products like a professional. If you're shy at sales, this book will give you the confidence you need to succeed.

Even seasoned salespeople will find tips and tricks in this book that will make them more effective and successful. Who is this book for? The answer is simple: this book is for you!

Smile is, quite simply, the fastest, easiest, most cost-effective investment you can make to surprise and delight your customers and create a profitable business or career. Now get out there and smile!

HOW TO GET THE MOST OUT OF THIS BOOK

The Top Ten

This book begins with the "Top Ten" of customer service and sales techniques. If you take away nothing else from this book, these 10 powerful techniques will help you transform your relationship with customers and increase sales. You'll learn how easy it is to surprise and delight your customers, make them smile from ear to ear, and keep them coming back.

More Amazing Service and Sales Techniques

The remainder of the book builds on the Top Ten, offering additional tips to help you give great service (Keep Them Smiling), increase sales (Sell More), handle difficult sales situations (When There's a Problem), and build customer loyalty (Create a Customer for Life). If you take the tips and techniques in these chapters to heart, your sales and customer service success will skyrocket. Trust me — it really works!

How to Use This Book

This book is the result of over 30 years of sales and customer service experience. If the ideas are new to you, you may want to take some time to digest and practice each chapter before moving on to the next. If you already have a strong background in customer service or sales, you can use this book as a refresher course or reference tool. You can read straight through or consult the Table of Contents to find the tips you most need to work on.

If you're using this book to train new employees or current staff, choose one or two concepts to highlight and practice each day or each week. If your staff is more seasoned, you may want to have them review the book as a whole before zeroing in on the concepts you most need to work on given your industry or service sector and your own unique challenges.

Make It Stick
It's astonishing how quickly we forget things. Whether you're an employer or an employee, take a few minutes each month to review this book so the best practices presented here become habit. This will keep you sharp — and keep your customers delighted!

1

THE
TOP
TEN

HOW TO MAKE
YOUR CUSTOMERS
SMILE (AND BUY!)

SMILE

When a customer enters your business or office, greet them promptly and politely — just as you would greet a guest in your home.

Here's How

1. **Smile.** Make it a warm, genuine, heartfelt smile.
2. **Look your customer in the eye and say "Hello!"** Speak in a warm, upbeat, and friendly manner.

This may sound basic, but you'd be surprised how many businesses fail to greet their customers properly.

According to Malcolm Gladwell, author of *Blink,* **first impressions occur instantaneously or within two seconds.** A simple smile and friendly "Hello" are extremely powerful and can mean the difference between a customer spending their money with you (and possibly becoming a customer for life) and walking out the door to spend it with your competition.

> Indifference is one of the biggest reasons people don't return to a business.

The Smile Study

In *The New York Times* bestseller *Buyology,* Martin Lindstrom discusses "The Smile Study." Its bottom line? A smile from a salesperson leads to more sales.

Is your business smiling? A positive first impression sets the tone and dynamics for all future interactions and transactions. It can make all the difference in the world in increasing sales and transforming customer service!

A man without a smiling face must not open a shop.
FAMOUS CHINESE PROVERB

MAKE A FRIEND

People buy from people they like and trust — from friends — so it's important to remember the golden rule: **Treat people the way you'd like to be treated.** Be nice, be polite, and don't be afraid to approach a customer to initiate an exchange. Make a friend!

Here's How

1. Greet your customer properly (with a genuine smile and a warm "Hello!").

2. Engage them in an initial short and friendly conversation. Find out how they're doing: **"It's nice to see you. How's your day going?"** When appropriate, give a genuine compliment: **"I really like your sweater."**

> Shoppers who interact more with employees spend more money.

3. *Then* find out how you can help them: **"What exactly brings you in today?"** or **"How can I help you?"**

REMEMBER As you build friendly relationships with your customers, you differentiate yourself and your company from your competition — and you're well on your way to creating a customer for life!

A stranger is just a friend I haven't met yet.
WILL ROGERS

3

ANSWER THE PHONE WITH A SMILE

When you answer the phone at your place of business, you're the first point of contact with your prospects and customers. It's critical that you make a great first impression.

How do you find the right tone? It's simple — **smile as you answer the phone.**

You may not realize it, but a smile totally changes the tone of your voice and "shines through" the phone line. Try it and you'll see — your happy, smiling voice will delight your customers and create a positive impression of you and your business!

Here's How

1. Smile and say: **"Good morning (or afternoon or evening)!"** Be sure to speak clearly.
2. State the complete name of your business, or say: **"Welcome to _____ [your complete business name]."**
3. Say: **"This is _____ [your name]. How may I help you?"**

Be upbeat, warm, inviting, and genuine — greet customers just as you would greet a guest in your home.

> When your initial encounter with a customer is over the phone, 70% of how you're perceived is based solely on the tone of your voice.

A Typical Greeting

Let's use the example of a hypothetical company called Burton's Chocolates. When the phone rings, here's how most businesses answer:

"Burton's Chocolates!"

If you were a customer on the other end of the line, looking to spend your hard-earned dollars on a gift for someone you love, how would this greeting make you feel?

The Right Way

Now, let's try it the right way:

"Good afternoon (or "Good morning" or "Good evening"), Burton's Chocolates. This is Pam. How may I help you?"

See and feel the difference?

In the first example, it's as if the company doesn't care about you. You may not even feel like you're being greeted (because you're not). The second greeting, by contrast, draws you in with a warm and professional welcome. It feels as if the person answering the phone is eager to serve you. Which business would *you* rather call?

Here are a few other pointers for amazing customer service over the phone:

1. Try to answer the phone within two rings, and definitely within three.

2. Call the customer by name when possible.

3. Always thank the customer for calling.

"Small stuff" matters. A lot!
TOM PETERS, AUTHOR OF *THE LITTLE BIG THINGS*

4

SAY PLEASE AND THANK YOU

Say **"Please"** when you request something from a customer. For example, **"May I please have your address?"** or **"Could you please tell me your suit size?"**

Say **"Thank you"** when a customer makes a purchase, when you're finishing up a phone call with a customer, or any time it's appropriate. Remember, customers are the reason you get paid. Graciously acknowledge this fact in all your dealings with them, whether in person, over the phone, or online.

> Lack of gratitude is one of the main reasons donors stop contributing to a charity.

When a customer leaves your business, thank them for coming in. Simply say "Thank you!" in a warm and genuine manner. Or try **"Thank you for coming in!"** or **"Thank you so much for stopping by — we look forward to seeing you again soon!"**

Keep it professional. Don't say "Have a good one," "Take care," "See you next time," or "Later."

Say "You're Welcome"

And when a customer says "Thank you," answer with a smile and a polite **"You're welcome."** Don't answer with "Sure," "No problem," or "Yep." Always treat your customer with the utmost respect.

Two examples come to mind. Recently I picked up my dog from doggie day care. After I paid, I said "Thank you" to the employee at the register, not really expecting a response. He smiled, made eye contact, and said **"You're welcome."** This simple gesture made me feel great. I made a mental note to come back to this business and tell my friends about it.

In another example, a friendly employee at a local business thanked me as I was leaving and then added, **"Have a wonderful day!"** It made me feel terrific and look forward to coming back.

How often does this kind of thing happen? Not often enough, unfortunately. You can make it happen every time you deal with a customer!

**The end result of kindness
is that it draws people to you.**
ANITA RODDICK, FOUNDER
OF THE BODY SHOP

5

ACKNOWLEDGE NEW CUSTOMERS — EVEN WHEN YOU'RE BUSY

How many times have you walked into a business and been ignored? There are countless stories of people waiting around at a store or business fully intending to make a purchase and many times a substantial one. After failing to be acknowledged, they simply leave and spend their money elsewhere. Don't let this happen to you!

If you're busy with a customer and someone else comes in, **immediately acknowledge the new customer.**

Here's How

1. Smile.
2. Greet the new customer with a warm **"Hello!"**
3. Look them in the eye and say: **"I'll be right with you"** or **"I'll be with you in a few minutes, as soon as I finish up with my customer."**

> Seventy percent of small business customers will leave and buy from someone else if they feel the sales staff doesn't care.

Then, when you *do* get to them, say: **"Thank you so much for waiting! What exactly can I help you with today?"**

Or, if you know you're going to be tied up for a while, say: **"Hello, I'm with a customer, let me get someone to assist you."** Then excuse yourself for a moment with your current customer and find someone to help the new customer.

And if you're working with more than one customer at a time and need to check in with someone else, excuse yourself briefly by saying, **"Excuse me for a moment — I'm just going to check on another customer. I'll be right back."**

You'll find that, in most cases, *both* customers will be impressed with your service!

Everyone has an invisible sign hanging from their neck saying, "Make me feel important." Never forget this message when working with people.
MARY KAY ASH, FOUNDER OF MARY KAY

6

NEVER ASK "CAN I HELP YOU?"

When a customer enters your business, **never ask "Can I help you?"** Why? Because it's too easy for them to say "No" and end the interaction.

"Can I help you?" is a **closed-ended question,** one that a customer can answer with a simple "Yes" or "No."

Closed-ended questions usually start with the word **"Can"** ("Can I help you with something?"), **"Is"** ("Is there anything I can help you with today?"), **"Do,"** or **"Did"** ("Do/Did you need any help?").

Instead, ask your customer an **open-ended question,** such as:

"How can I help you?"

"What can I help you with today?"

"What exactly are you looking for today?"

Open-ended questions usually begin with **"Who," "What," "When," "Where," "Why,"** or **"How."**

Open-ended questions can't be answered with "No." They encourage customers to provide you with detailed and specific information about their wants and needs.

UNCOVER YOUR CUSTOMER'S ULTIMATE BUYING MOTIVE

The key to sales is to **uncover your customer's Ultimate Buying Motive (UBM).** This is the main problem they're trying to solve — the one thing that's keeping them up at night. It's the reason they've come into your business in the first place.

What's in It for Me? (WIIFM)

Remember, the customer only cares about "What's in it for me" — a well-known business maxim. Always keep this in mind. Focus not on making the sale, but on meeting your customer's needs and wants, and you *will* make the sale.

> Only 38% of salespeople understand their prospects' needs and how their product can help.

Once you understand your customer's UBM, show how your product or service will help them address it. Be certain to verbalize exactly how your product will help them solve their problem.

What It Looks Like

Salesperson: "Hello, what can I help you with today?"

Customer: "I want to buy a cell phone for my mother."

Salesperson: "What type of phone are you looking for?"

Customer: "My mother is 85 years old, and I want her to be able to call me in an emergency. Her eyesight is bad, though — I don't think she'd be able to read most cell phones. I need something dependable, too. I need to know it'll work when she needs it."

Salesperson: "Based on what you're telling me, I'd recommend our 'Easy View' model. It's the model with the largest buttons. They're very easy for people with weak eyesight to see, so she'll definitely be able to read the numbers and call you whenever she needs to. It's also very reliable — all our phones get top marks for dependability. Does that sound like what you're looking for?"

Customer: "Absolutely!"

Notice that the salesperson in this example does a great job focusing on the customer's UBM, only talking about the features that they care about and that will help them solve their problem (large buttons and dependable service), without mentioning things that don't matter to the customer (like texting capability or data plans).

REMEMBER Your job is to direct your customer toward the product or service that best fulfills their needs and wants. A customer whose needs are met will not only be happy and ready to purchase, but eager to return to your business and recommend it to others!

Stop selling. Start helping.
ZIG ZIGLAR, AUTHOR, SALESPERSON,
AND MOTIVATIONAL SPEAKER

8

PROBE (ASK QUESTIONS)

Once a customer tells you what they're looking for, **probe, or dig deeper, with a series of relevant questions** to learn more about their problem (or Ultimate Buying Motive). Then be quiet and listen as they tell you what they want and need in order to solve it.

Ask specific open-ended questions (remember, open-ended questions usually begin with "Who," "What," "When," "Where," "Why," or "How") to uncover, layer by layer, your customer's needs and preferences.

What It Looks Like

Customer: "I'm looking for a new chainsaw."

Salesperson: "I'll be happy to help you. Who is the chainsaw for?" (*This is an important question. I can't tell you how many times I've assumed the person buying the product or service was buying it for themselves only to discover later that they were buying it for someone else with totally different needs! My failure to clarify up front meant I had to start my questioning over, wasting my customer's time, and mine.*)

> The best salespeople are more naturally curious than their less successful counterparts.

Customer: "My wife."

Salesperson: "What's she planning to use it for?"

Customer: "To cut branches in the woods outside our house."

Salesperson: "Does she have a chainsaw now?" (*Another important question: learning about a currently or previously owned product is a direct route to a wealth of information about your customer's wants, needs, and the product they seek.*)

Customer: "Yes."

Salesperson: "Could you please tell me a little bit about the chainsaw she has now and what she likes and doesn't like about it?"

Customer: "Sure. The chainsaw she has works fine but it's too heavy for her to carry for a long time, and she doesn't like mixing the gas and oil. She heard that Stihl makes an electric chainsaw. Can you tell me anything about that?"

Salesperson: "Sure. The Stihl electric chainsaw is lighter weight than a gas chainsaw, so it'll be light enough for your wife to carry all day long. And it doesn't require gas or engine oil, so she won't have to worry about mixing them anymore. How does that sound?"

Customer: "It sounds perfect!"

LISTEN

One of the most valuable lessons you can learn from this book is to **LISTEN** to your customers. Ask probing questions — then **listen attentively** to your customer's answers.

Listening builds trust. If your customer feels that you care and aren't just trying to sell them something, they'll be more open to your buying suggestions later on. Listening makes you more credible in the eyes of your customer.

> Even in a tough economy, 60% of customers will pay more for a better service experience.

To be certain you can retain the important information your customer is giving you, feel free to take notes as they're speaking. And to be sure you've heard them properly, acknowledge or repeat back to them what they've said and ask them to confirm:

> **"If I understand you correctly,** you're telling me that your wife wants a lighter weight chainsaw because her current chainsaw is too heavy, that she wants to cut branches with it, and that she doesn't like mixing gas and oil. **Is that correct?"**

Then, be a problem solver. Listening will help you understand your customer's problem — the next step is to show how your product or service can help them solve it. Always provide a solution to your customer's problem, emphasizing what matters most to them:

"We have a great product that's **lighter weight, works great on branches, and doesn't require any mixing of fuel.** It also offers a 30-day warranty, so you can try it out with no risk involved."

Biggest Sales Mistake

All too often, salespeople make the mistake of not listening to their customer. Without asking any qualifying questions or giving the customer a chance to speak, many immediately launch into a boring, irrelevant product presentation.

They "product dump" — telling the customer everything there is to know about their product or service, regardless of whether the customer cares about what it is they're describing.

Not only is this unhelpful, but it can actually turn the customer off. As Katya Andresen notes in *Robin Hood Marketing,* "People don't need to know everything; they simply want to know what is immediately relevant to them."

TIP You can show you're listening by making good eye contact and nodding your head periodically while your customer is talking.

We're all learning here; the best listeners will end up the smartest.
CHARLENE LI AND JOSH BERNOFF,
AUTHORS OF *GROUNDSWELL*

10

KNOW YOUR PRODUCT — AND YOUR COMPETITION

Know the features and benefits of your product or service. Learn everything you can about it, and know your business, industry, and customers, as well. This includes knowing business hours, pricing, and procedures by heart.

Regularly review relevant trade journals, brochures, manuals, newsletters, websites, and social media sites to keep yourself up to speed on your product or service. Be aware of any significant awards it has won. Have positive quotes from the media and testimonials from past or current customers ready to share.

While you'll learn a lot from research and from satisfied customers, ultimately the best way to know your product or service is to use it yourself if possible. Your own experience will be a powerful testimonial to your customers and give you an insider's edge in promoting the product and answering questions.

Finally, don't just get to know your own products and services — **study your competitor's, as well.** Know the strengths and weaknesses of your competition and how its products or services stack up against your own.

Keep It Positive

Never present your competition in a negative light, even though you may have the information to do so. Saying something negative about a competing business, product, or service is often viewed as very unprofessional by customers. Instead, simply lay out the information for your customer and let them decide.

If your customer tells you they like your service, but are leaning toward buying your competitor's, politely explain the differences between the two and the advantages of your own — without ever saying anything negative about your competitor's product, service, or place of business.

What It Looks Like

"I'm sure the business down the street is a fair place to do business. The advantage of our product is that it gives you six options for your insurance policy, so you'll be able to customize it to your liking. Like I said, the product our competitors provide is good, but it only offers two options. And, you know, it's good to have choices when it comes to insurance."

OR

"Our service offers an additional year of warranty — which adds up to more security and peace of mind."

REMEMBER Knowing your product or service inside and out will make *you* the expert and give you the confidence you need to help your customer choose what's right for them.

I can't think of a greater dissatisfier than lack of product knowledge when it comes to customer satisfaction and retention.
ANGELA MEGASKO, PRESIDENT AND CEO OF MARKET VIEWPOINT

2

KEEP THEM SMILING

MORE TOP CUSTOMER SERVICE TECHNIQUES

MAKE GOOD EYE CONTACT

Eye contact is one of the best ways to make a positive impression. Good eye contact conveys respect, confidence, competence, honesty, and interest, making it easy for your customer to like and trust you.

Here's How
Look your customer in the eye when you're talking with them. Don't stare, but don't let your eyes wander to look at other customers or anything else, either.

TIP If you feel like you're staring, look at your customer's nose (no joke!). You can also blink, nod your head, and smile from time to time to break things up.

YOUR BODY SPEAKS

Your body speaks, and your customers are listening! Whether you're helping a customer in your store, working with a client in your office, or staffing a booth at a trade show, be aware of how you're carrying yourself and interacting with your customer. **Make sure your body language is welcoming and professional.**

Here's How

1. **Smile and maintain good eye contact.** Send the message that you're eager to be of service at any time.
2. **Look alert and approachable.** Stand whenever possible and leave your arms open at your sides (not crossed). Be sure to stand up straight.
3. **Respect your customer's space.** Get a sense of their comfort zone by observing the distance they stand in proximity to you — then follow their lead.
4. **Keep it professional.** Don't touch your customer unless you're shaking hands.

> Sixty to sixty-five percent of communication is nonverbal.

CALL THE CUSTOMER BY NAME

People love hearing their name! One of the best ways to make a favorable impression on a customer or client is to **call them by name.**

Here's How
1. If you don't know your customer, look them in the eye and introduce yourself by name (if it's appropriate to your business) and wait for them to respond with their own name.
2. If your customer doesn't give their name, feel free to ask for it by saying, **"And you are?"**
3. Then shake their hand firmly and enthusiastically say: **"It's a pleasure to meet you, _____."**

For example, start an interaction with **"What can I do for you today, Mr. Johnson?"**

Or when finishing up a transaction with a client, say: **"Thank you for signing up with our firm to handle your company's 401(k) plan, Ms. Tyson."**

Introducing yourself sets the stage for a successful interaction and a long-term personal relationship — remember, people buy from friends!

A person's name is to that person the sweetest and most important sound in any language.
DALE CARNEGIE, AUTHOR OF *HOW TO WIN FRIENDS AND INFLUENCE PEOPLE*

BE ENTHUSIASTIC

Have you ever done business with people who lack enthusiasm and seem totally uninterested, unexcited, or just plain dull? If you have, you know the difference enthusiasm makes. When you deal with an enthusiastic salesperson or representative, the sales process is fun and engaging. Their enthusiasm is contagious, and you feel like you've made a lifelong friend.

Be the person you'd want to be dealing with if you were in your customer's shoes. Your enthusiasm, positive attitude, and interest in helping your customers will leave them delighted and help you sell more. And that's not all — approaching your job, and your life, with enthusiasm will bring energy, fun, and satisfaction for *you,* as well!

All top salespeople like themselves and love their work. And their customers can feel it. As a result, their customers want to buy from them, buy from them again, and recommend them to their friends.
BRIAN TRACY, AUTHOR OF *BE A SALES SUPERSTAR*

DRESS FOR SUCCESS

Always dress appropriately for your industry and strive to match your appearance to customer expectations. People form an opinion of you within the first few seconds of meeting you, and yes, they do judge a book by its cover. Make sure your dress is in keeping with the professional image of your company, whether on the job or at an event.

Always overdress a bit to err on the side of looking professional. Keep your clothes clean and neat, and ironed if necessary. Keep your shoes in nice condition. Make sure any jewelry is appropriate to your business.

Pay attention to your grooming, as well — in most situations, a neatly groomed, clean-shaven look is best.

REMEMBER A professional, well-groomed look will add to your credibility and help you sell more!

KEEP IT PROFESSIONAL

Never talk with other employees about non-business matters, talk with friends and family on your cell phone, or text when customers are present. Many customers will see this as a sign of disrespect.

Be aware that customers can often hear you even when they're out of sight. Patients in a waiting room or customers in line at a post office or agency will often be able to hear you talking in back even if you can't see them. Save personal interactions for situations where customers can't see or hear you or for after hours.

REMEMBER You represent your company, and everything you say and do can be observed!

DON'T MAKE THE CUSTOMER WAIT

Most people hate to wait, whether at the doctor's or dentist's office, in line at the bank, or for someone to complete a transaction in a store or over the phone.

If you work in customer service or sales, always keep an eye out for customers who are waiting. If you have time and they haven't been assisted, **jump in and see how you can help.**

If the customer is already being taken care of, find out who's helping them and ask that person if there's anything you can do to assist them to make the transaction go faster — often, there is!

> Two in three customers have walked out of a store in the past year because of poor customer service.

Keep Lines Short

In *Why We Buy,* Paco Underhill calls wait time "the single most important factor in customer satisfaction." He gives the following example:

> *One housewares chain's vice president was startled when we showed him video in which a woman who had just spent twenty-two minutes shopping in his store joined a very long checkout line, stood there until it dawned on her that she was in cashier hell, and abandoned her full cart and exited the place.*

Don't let this happen to you! When you have more than

one customer in line, **ring for a backup cashier** to swiftly move customers on their way. Follow Target's lead — when they have three or more customers waiting, they open up another checkout lane to keep things "Fast, Fun, and Friendly."

At my own retail store, customer-centered teamwork was store policy. Employees would help bag items for the person ringing up a sale to make the transaction go that much faster. And if we had more than one person in the checkout line, cashiers would ring a special buzzer to bring extra employees to the front.

Customers loved the extra attention and were delighted to get out the door sooner. They left on a happy note, which made it much more likely they'd be back!

Make the customer the hero of your story.

ANN HANDLEY, ONLINE MARKETING EXPERT
AND AUTHOR OF *CONTENT RULES*

HOLD PLEASE: ASK PERMISSION FIRST

When you're on the phone with a customer and need to put them on hold, it's another opportunity to make them smile!

Here's How
Before you place your customer on hold:
1. **Ask for permission.**
2. **Let them know how long they can expect to wait.**
3. **Thank them for holding.**

If the wait will be long, ask if they'd prefer that you call them back.

What It Looks Like
You: "Could I please place you on hold for two minutes so I can find the answer for you?"

Customer: "Certainly."

You: "Thank you for holding — I'll be right back with your answer."

Then, when you return to the phone, say: **"Thank you again for holding."**

If you're going to have to unexpectedly leave your customer on hold longer than expected, whether they're waiting for you or for someone else, simply pick up the phone and inform them:

> **"I'm sorry — I told you I'd have the answer to your question in two minutes, but it's actually going to take me a few more minutes to find your answer. Could I please put you on hold for**

a few more minutes, or would you prefer that I take your number and call you back?"

Finally, if your business is busy, like a pizza place on a Friday night, be careful not to cut corners. Don't just answer the phone with:

"Joe's Pizza, can you please hold?"

Instead, give your customer a proper introduction first, and *then* ask permission to put them on hold:

"Good evening, Joe's Pizza. This is Susan speaking. May I please put you on hold?"

No matter how busy you are, you must take time to make the other person feel important.
MARY KAY ASH, FOUNDER OF MARY KAY

WHEN THE PHONE RINGS WHILE YOU'RE WITH A CUSTOMER

If you need to answer the phone while you're busy with a customer, put your current customer first.

Here's How

1. **Excuse yourself** with your current customer before you answer the phone.
2. **Thank the person who's calling** for contacting you and **politely explain that you're already helping a customer or client.**
3. **Ask for their name and phone number** and repeat the number back to them to verify that you've written it down correctly.
4. **Tell them you'll call them back** — don't talk to the caller at length and leave your customer waiting.

   Once you've finished assisting your initial customer, call your phone customer back right away and thank

> In the past year, one in two customers have walked away from an intended purchase due to poor customer service.

them for their patience. If you don't have time to call them back immediately, hand the name and number to a co-worker and ask them to call — then follow up to make certain they did!

FOLLOW UP

Follow-up is key to providing amazing customer service and making sales. Always **follow up promptly with customers and provide timely updates and communications.**

Phone

Return phone calls right away — at least by the end of the business day, at worst within 24 hours.

Email

The rule for email is exactly the same: return all email inquiries from customers as soon as possible — at least by the end of the business day, at worst within 24 hours.

Service Situations

If you're an automotive or other service business with a waiting room, keep your customers informed on the status of their repair on a consistent basis, perhaps hourly. Don't leave them wondering or feeling disrespected or ignored.

Similarly, if you're managing a waiting room or examination rooms in a health care setting, come back often to inform your patient on the status of their visit and how long they can expect to wait for test results or to see a doctor or nurse.

Sixty percent of millionaires cite not returning phone calls promptly as the top reason they'd fire a financial advisor.

If the customer is waiting off site, e.g. for car or computer repair, consistent updates are still very important. Let your customer know when they can expect to hear from you and follow through with regular updates.

TIP In all situations, a good rule of thumb is to always **do what you say you're going to do.** If you promise someone you'll "call them right back" or "get right back to them," then do it! Many businesses neglect this simple rule and lose many customers as a result.

SPECIAL ORDERS: MAKE THE CUSTOMER FEEL SPECIAL

When a customer places a special order, **follow up with a phone call or email once a week — or for urgent matters, once or twice a day or even hourly.**

Always keep your customer updated on the status of their order, unless they request otherwise. Then, as soon as the customer's order is ready, **contact them immediately.**

Seventy percent of customers are willing to spend more with companies that provide excellent customer service.

REMEMBER Special orders are an opportunity to stand out from your competition and make your customers smile. A well-handled special order can create a customer for life!

A customer is the most important visitor on our premises. He is not dependent on us. We are dependent on him... We are not doing him a favor by serving him. He is doing us a favor by giving us the opportunity to do so.
MAHATMA GANDHI

MASTER ELECTRONIC ETIQUETTE

Presentation is everything, even when using electronic media. An email is not a text message — it's a professional means of communication and should be treated as such. Emails to customers, prospects, vendors, etc., should use **proper English, full sentences, proper grammar and punctuation, and a suitable and specific subject line.**

They should also contain a **proper salutation and closing,** as well as an **email signature** with your first and last name, and the name, address, telephone number, and website of your company or organization.

Be sure to proofread and spell-check every email you write before sending it.

REMEMBER Every communication you send is a representation of you and your company or organization. Regardless of the purpose of your message, make sure it's professional and reflects well on you!

GIVE CHANGE CAREFULLY

When you give a customer change, first **make eye contact and smile.** Then **present the change so the customer can easily handle it and put it in their wallet or purse.**

Place the coins in their hand first, then the dollar bills. Many people put the coins *on top* of the dollar bills. This can cause the change to slide off and fall to the floor.

Count out the amount of the change as you place the coins and bills in your customer's hand. As you present the bills to your customer, make sure they're all face up and facing the same way.

What It Looks Like

You: "Your change is $16.37 — that's 25, 35, and 37 (*as you place the quarter, dime, and two pennies in their hand*), and 10, 15, and 16 (*as you place the ten, five, and one dollar bill in their hand*)."

Make eye contact and smile when you're done counting out the change. Finish by saying **"Thank you!"**

3

SELL MORE

MORE SECRETS TO SUCCESSFUL SELLING

DON'T POINT — WALK AND SHOW (AND SELL!)

When a customer asks you where something is located in your business, don't point to the location or aisle or just tell them the aisle number.

Instead, **walk the customer to the exact location and show them the exact product or service they're looking for.**

Then let them know about any noteworthy benefits the product may have, any customer testimonials or credible news stories that might help promote it, or any other relevant information that might assist them in making their decision. Remember, this is a prime opportunity for you to help your customer with their purchase.

For example, **"This brand was voted the top interior paint in a recent survey by *Consumer Reports*."** If the customer is considering more than one product or service, this is also a great opportunity to **ask and answer questions** and **help explain any important differences** between the products they're considering.

Consumers cite knowledgeable staff and polite and friendly employees as the most important areas of customer service.

This is a fairly simple point, but businesses often miss the mark. I was in a major hardware chain store near my hometown recently, and I approached a clerk and said "Hello." He grunted. I asked him if they carried wire and he said "Yeah." I asked him where it was and he pointed somewhere down a huge maze of aisles. I asked him which aisle it was in, and he grunted again, "Aisle 5." Needless to say, I was not impressed! Don't be this guy!

REMEMBER When you handle the basics of selling well, not only will your customers want to buy, but they'll be eager to return to you the next time they have a problem or need.

When the customer comes first, the customer will last.
ROBERT HALF, FOUNDER OF ROBERT HALF INTERNATIONAL

"JUST LOOKING": LET THEM BROWSE AND SHOP

When someone tells you they're "Just looking," let them browse. Don't intimidate them by walking toward them and trying to initiate an immediate sale. Instead, stand in place or even walk backward a bit.

The idea is to **make them more anxious to buy than you are to sell** — something my uncle Gene, an expert salesman, taught me.

Communicate to your customer that you'll be available if and when they need help, but don't pressure them. You can set up the expectation that you'll be back by saying, **"Great! Look around. My name is _____, and I'll check back with you in a bit to see if you have any questions."** This keeps the door open for further communication.

As your customer continues to look around, take care not to hover. Some people genuinely want to browse on their own, and they may get turned off and leave if you're too assertive. Check in on them from a distance from time to time to watch for signs (such as eye contact) that they're looking for help.

If your co-worker has just asked a customer if they need help and they've said they prefer to browse on their own, don't be a pest and also ask them if they need help. Only approach them if you have a clear sign that they've changed their mind.

More Than "Just Looking"

Sometimes customers will react automatically and say "Just looking" out of habit when you offer to help them. If you feel strongly that your customer is not "Just looking" and is truly interested in making a purchase, you might be more assertive and say something like:

> **"You're more than welcome to look around. I'm happy to guide you in the right direction, then let you browse on your own. What in particular are you looking for?"**

OR

> **"What exactly are you looking for? Maybe I can guide you in the right direction."**

This will give you the opportunity to walk them to the product they're most interested in and find out whether they'd like further assistance when they get there.

LOOK FOR BUYING SIGNALS

When a customer is ready to buy, you can expect to see **buying signals.** Different customers will give different cues, but **most people will show some type of sign as they move closer to making a purchase.**

Being aware of buying signals will help you meet the individual shopping needs of each of your customers. You'll be able to move in and offer assistance when it's appropriate and give your customer space when it's not.

HERE ARE SOME SIGNS THAT A CUSTOMER IS READY TO BUY:

- They will make long eye contact with you.
- They will look for someone to help them.
- They will spend quite a bit of time studying one product or service.
- They will ask you about the product.
- They will ask what type of payments you accept — "Do you accept credit cards?"
- They will ask about price — "Is this item on sale?" or "Will this item be going on sale soon?"
- They will compare two or several products, looking from one to the other or holding them in their hands.
- They will ask your opinion or another person's opinion about the product.
- They will look inside their wallet or purse.

HERE ARE SOME SIGNS THAT A CUSTOMER IS *NOT* READY TO BUY:

- They will avoid eye contact with you.
- They will tell you (with certainty in their voice) that they're "Just looking."
- They will look at a range of different items (browsing rather than looking intently at a particular product or type of product).

TIP Keep an eye on customers who are "not yet ready to buy" as they may become "ready to buy" soon! Watch for signs of customers zeroing in on a single product or section of the store or weighing one product against another.

FEATURES TELL, BENEFITS SELL

Be very clear on the difference between features and benefits. **Features are characteristics of a product or service,** like an anti-glare screen on a cell phone, front suspension on a bike, or Automatic Crash Response on a vehicle.

BENEFITS GO DEEPER — THEY'RE WHAT A PRODUCT OR SERVICE WILL DO FOR THE CUSTOMER TO MEET HIS OR HER NEEDS AND WANTS:

- An anti-glare screen will allow your customer to read their cell phone display outdoors.

- Front suspension will absorb bumps when biking over rough surfaces — this may be especially important if your customer has a wrist injury or arthritis.

- Automatic Crash Response will give your customer peace of mind knowing that emergency services will be notified immediately when an accident occurs, regardless of whether the driver is able to call for help.

When communicating with a customer, be sure to make the link between features and benefits. Features are great to know about, but what matters most to a customer is what a product will do for them. **Always direct your customer's attention to benefits, or how a product will help them solve their problem.**

What It Looks Like

Customer: "My leg gets sore on long drives."

Salesperson: "This car has adaptive cruise control **[this is a feature]**. What this means to you is that you can set the cruise control while you're driving and take your foot off the gas pedal to give your leg a rest on long drives **[this is a benefit]**."

TIP Saying **"What this means to you..."** or **"This means..."** after you name a feature provides an easy transition into explaining its benefits.

One of the biggest marketing mistakes is to talk about features like horsepower when your customers only care about benefits like getting home for dinner.
GEORGE TOROK, AUTHOR OF *SECRETS OF POWER MARKETING*

CONTROL THE SALE

Remember that, in most cases, you know more about your products and services than your customer. You're the expert, so it's only appropriate that you control the direction and pace of the sale or service issue.

Ask questions and listen carefully to understand your customer's specific needs and concerns — then **be ready to take the lead, showing confidence and initiating the next step in the sales process, as appropriate.**

What It Looks Like

Customer: "I'm still thinking about ordering, but I'm just not ready."

You: "Tanya, I know you've been thinking about ordering for a few months now. Is there a particular reason you're waiting?"

Customer: "No, I just want to make sure I'm making the right decision."

You: "Based on everything you've told me, it seems like this product is exactly what you've been looking for. It's also in your price range, and you like the service and warranty. Are there any other questions I can answer for you?"

Customer: "No, you've answered all my questions. I just hate to jump into this — I'd like to think about it some more."

You: "Tanya, I'll tell you what. I know this product could make a real difference for you. Why don't you use our financing and you can get started using it — how does that sound?"

Customer: "How much would I need to put down?"

You: "We only need 30% down."

Customer: "That *does* sound workable… Okay, let's do it!"

Above all, the most important thing is to **be respectful and professional throughout the interaction, even as you're taking control.** Be polite and show that you're doing your best to help — this will make it easy for the customer to follow your lead.

TIP One way to have more success in controlling the sale is to **mirror the customer's personality.** For example, if your customer is talking slowly, *you* talk slowly — if your customer is talking fast, *you* talk fast. This works because people tend to like people who remind them of themselves. Mirroring their personality puts them at ease.

ANSWER OBJECTIONS

Sometimes customers will raise an objection in the course of the sales process, telling you they're unwilling or unable to buy. It's important to understand that **an objection is not a rejection** — it's a temporary roadblock. Your job is to acknowledge it and remove it.

Be aware that an objection may reflect a possible misunderstanding on the part of the customer. They may have false or insufficient information about a product or service or may not understand its features and benefits.

Often objections are based on problems the customer has had in the past with similar products or companies. They may just want to make sure they won't have the same problem with your product or service, or with you.

The Objection Is an Opportunity

By raising the objection, your customer has provided you with valuable information. You now have a much better understanding of what's keeping them from purchasing your product, and you can use this information to continue the customer along in the sales process.

View the objection as an opportunity. Respond with your own knowledge and professional salesmanship — now clearly targeted at one of the customer's main barriers to purchase.

For example, if the customer objects to the price of a product or service, perceiving it as "too expensive," explain the features and benefits that warrant the higher price. Perhaps the item is of higher quality — in the case of a mutual fund, for example, it may offer a more experienced fund manager. **These and all features and benefits need to be explained to your customer.**

What It Looks Like

Customer: "I can buy this cheaper online from a discount site."

Salesperson: "I totally understand your concern about costs. You told me you need the product by tomorrow, though, and if you buy from us, you can have it today. If you buy online, you won't get the product for a few days unless you pay overnight shipping, and that can be very expensive. Regardless of how it's shipped, shipping and handling fees could easily eat up any cost savings. Plus we stand behind what we sell, and returns are a snap since we're right here in town."

Customer: "You know, you're right. It makes more sense to just get it here. Can I pay by credit card?"

Customer: "I'm not interested in this model — I heard it was built for women."

Salesperson: "Actually, Bill, a lot of men buy this car and love it. You're right, it *was* designed with women's needs in mind, but it handles great and half the people who buy it are men. You really should give it a test drive."

Customer: "Okay, I'll give it a shot."

Always take your customer's objections seriously and answer them to the best of your ability, in a friendly and helpful manner. Give your customer all the information they need to understand the value, and the price, of your product or service.

TIP **Try to anticipate the objections your customer is most likely to raise and be prepared ahead of time with an appropriate answer for each.** This will make it easy for you to respond quickly and effectively the moment an objection is raised.

An objection is often a way for the prospect to say "Tell me more."
MARC PITMAN, FUNDRAISING EXPERT
AND AUTHOR OF *ASK WITHOUT FEAR!*

OVERCOME THE FEAR OF SELLING: ASK FOR THE SALE (OR DONATION)

It's normal to have some fear when it comes to selling. Whether you're new to sales or you've been at it for years, it can be easy to feel like you might be bothering a customer or pushing something on them.

Instead of thinking of what you're doing as selling, think of it as **helping the customer buy what they need.** After all, if they didn't need your product or service, they wouldn't be contacting you in the first place.

Imagine how grateful you feel when you're shopping for something you need and find someone who's helpful and knowledgeable — that's all a good salesperson is!

You're doing the customer a disservice if you *don't* help them buy what they need. If you don't ask for the sale, they'll likely just go somewhere else to purchase the same product.

> In 85% of interactions with prospects, the salesperson fails to ask for the sale.

Remember, the customer has come to you to solve a problem. First, be clear on what your customer's problem is and what they're looking for. Then **make a definitive recommendation — ask for the sale.**

Here's How

1. Ask probing questions to learn more about your customer's problem, wants, and needs.

2. **Listen attentively** to the answers you receive.
3. **Guide your customer** to the best solution.

When you're ready to make a recommendation, use these words to set up what you're about to say: **"Based on what you're telling me, I'd recommend…"** This creates a direct link between your customer's need and the product or service you're suggesting.

What It Looks Like

Salesperson: "Based on what you're telling me, it sounds like you had a hybrid bike before but it was difficult to ride off road on trails. Is that correct?"

Customer: "Yes, that's right."

Salesperson: "In that case, I'd recommend a mountain bike. This is our Trek model. As you can see, it has wider tires with more aggressive tread. Something like this is going to be much more stable off road."

Customer: "Yeah — I can see how this would be a lot better on trails."

Salesperson: "The Trek model has all the features you mentioned you wanted — a comfortable seat, front shocks, disk brakes…" (*Listing the features the customer asked for that the model you're recommending has.*)

Customer: "It does seem like a good bike."

Salesperson: "Does it sound like something you'd like to go with?" (*Asking for the sale.*)

Customer: "It does. Could I pay by check?"

As you prepare to recommend a product or service to your customer, **don't be afraid of rejection or of hearing the word "No."** Don't be afraid to say, **"Would you like to buy it?"**

Would You Like to Join?

Whether you're a for-profit or nonprofit, this concept is extremely important. Years ago, as development director for a nonprofit organization, I worked an annual weekend trade show. The organization had worked this show before but had never received a single donation. I decided to use the show as a test to see the difference asking for the sale could make.

First thing Saturday morning a man walked up to our table and I spoke with him about our mission. He asked me the cost of membership and I told him it was $30. He turned away and I thought to myself, "This must be what happens all the time. This is why they haven't received any donations — they've never asked for the sale!"

> "Why did you give?" "Because I was asked."
>
> **FAMOUS FUNDRAISING SAYING**

The man had already started to walk away when I politely called out, "Would you like to join?" He turned around immediately, pulled out his wallet, and handed me his credit card — just like that! He went on to become an annual donor and increased his gift each year. That weekend I received a total of 16 donations, about one an hour, just by asking for the sale.

One final bit of advice — "Fake it till you make it," as the famous saying goes. **Don't be afraid to ask for the sale**

or donation, even if you may not feel ready. If you truly understand your customer's problem and your own products and services, you are the *perfect* person to guide them toward what they need.

We miss one hundred percent of the sales we don't ask for.
ZIG ZIGLAR, AUTHOR, SALESPERSON, AND MOTIVATIONAL SPEAKER

ASK FOR THE SALE — THEN SHUT UP

Once you ask for the sale, **be quiet**. Don't utter a sound. The first person to talk loses.

What It Looks Like

Salesperson: "Does this sound like something you'd like to buy?" or "Would you like to buy it?"

Then be quiet.

Customer: *(Silence for a few seconds as he or she thinks about it…)* "Do you take credit cards?"

Salesperson: "Yes. Would you like to pay with MasterCard or Visa?"

Then BE QUIET, even if it means there's silence for 30 seconds or more. This rule applies whether you're talking with a customer in person or on the phone. If you stay quiet, the customer is much more likely to answer with a positive purchasing statement.

Customer: "Visa. Here's my credit card."

We usually say too much. It makes us less persuasive.
KATYA ANDRESEN, NONPROFIT MARKETING EXPERT
AND AUTHOR OF *ROBIN HOOD MARKETING*

SUGGEST COMPLEMENTARY PRODUCTS

When a customer purchases your product or service, whether in person or over the phone, it's a good idea to **suggest complementary products that they may need in addition to what they're buying.** This is in keeping with the famous line from McDonald's: "Would you like fries with that?"

This practice is known as **suggestive selling.** If you don't do it, you're leaving money on the table and giving business to your competitors. If your customer needs something more, they may as well save themselves time and effort and get it from you. You're doing them a favor by reminding them — you do them a disservice if you don't.

In some cases, a complementary product may be necessary to enjoy the product they're purchasing. For example, your customer may not be aware that batteries don't come with the battery-operated toy they just bought for their child.

> Suggestive selling can increase sales by 15 to 150 percent.

If you don't let them know, they'll get home and realize — or worse yet discover Christmas morning — that they're missing something crucial. If this happens, they may blame you and your business, and it could cost you a customer.

Even when a complementary item isn't essential, you won't know whether a customer is interested unless you ask.

What It Looks Like

You: "Were you aware that we have a stuffed toy available based on the character in this book?"

Customer: "No, I wasn't."

You: "It's a 10-inch stuffed fawn with bendable legs that sells for $14.95. Would you like to add this beautiful plush toy to your order?"

Customer: "Yes, my daughter will love that!"

This technique becomes even more effective when paired with delightful customer service. Recently, I visited a Trader Joe's specialty store in Cleveland, Ohio. Trader Joe's is one of my favorite places to shop — I'm always delighted by their clean stores, enthusiastic staff, excellent product selection, and outstanding customer service. The store was packed as usual.

When I went to check out, the nice employee at the cash register made eye contact, smiled, and said a friendly "Hello!" Then she asked me how my evening was going.

When she noticed I was buying chocolate, she said, "Have you tried our peppermint chocolate? It's out of this world!" I thanked her for the information and picked up a box of the chocolate, which was located near the register. After taking a look, I decided she was right — I needed to try it. I ended up buying two boxes.

I left the store feeling satisfied and happy (and I was even happier after I tried the chocolate, which was excellent). I still spread the word to others about the great service at Trader Joe's (as I'm doing now). This wonderful employee combined suggestive selling with great customer service and the result was a happy, satisfied customer who is now a fan!

If there is something to gain and nothing to lose by asking, by all means ask!
W. CLEMENT STONE, BUSINESSMAN AND AUTHOR

PREPARE: THE "SIX P'S"

According to the Six P's, **Proper Preparation Prevents Pathetically Poor Performance.** If you follow this advice for everything you do in business and in life, you'll be way ahead of the pack.

Proper preparation means **having ready ahead of time everything your customer or client will need to make a well-informed purchase decision or complete their transaction.** Proper preparation will build your own confidence — and the confidence of your customer in you — leading to a successful transaction.

PROPER PREPARATION MEANS THAT YOU:

- Know your products and services, and your competitor's products and services, inside and out

- Have customer or media testimonials, relevant awards, and other pertinent information at the ready

- Anticipate objections and have answers prepared ahead of time

> Only one in six sales professionals are "extremely prepared" for a meeting with a new customer.

- Are in a service and selling mindset whenever you're on the sales floor or in contact with customers

If possible, also do research on *your customer* ahead of time. Find out anything you can about past purchase history, likes and dislikes, and needs and wants.

REMEMBER Anticipating anything that could get in the way of a sale — and making sure you have a powerful and effective backup plan — is the key to sales success!

Luck is preparation meeting opportunity.
OPRAH WINFREY

AVOID THE CURSE OF KNOWLEDGE

The **curse of knowledge** is when you know so much about your business and are so close to it that you're unable to relate to customers and communicate effectively with them about your product or service.

Avoid the curse of knowledge! Work hard to understand your customer's needs and wants, but also their knowledge of the topic at hand.

Here's How

Use words and concepts your customer will understand. Avoid industry jargon — it's like speaking a foreign language to your customer. Instead, translate your knowledge into layman's terms.

If you need to explain a condition or a problem, take time to do the issue justice. Use the word "like" in an analogy that your customer (or client or patient) can relate to, then ask them if they understand.

For example, **"A weak heart with a leaky valve is like your car tire with a slow leak — does that make sense?"**

My doctor did a great job of this recently when I came to him on a follow-up visit after being treated for bronchitis. He listened to my breathing for a second and immediately told me I was still fighting the bronchitis. I asked how he could tell so quickly, and he told me he could hear a wheezing sound in my lungs that was typical of bronchitis.

He then drew me a very detailed, easy-to-understand picture of bronchial tubes and the bronchitis. He explained everything in layman's terms that I understood. He reassured me that he knew how to treat the problem effectively and then laid out my treatment options. What a great experience! I left feeling respected and confident in my doctor and the treatment.

If your customer happens to be very familiar with the topic at hand and comfortable with industry terms, feel free to use technical language as appropriate. Some customers will prefer this.

REMEMBER When you communicate effectively, you dramatically increase the likelihood of a positive outcome or sale!

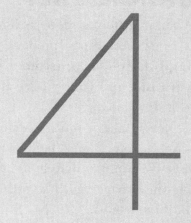

WHEN
THERE'S A
PROBLEM

TURNING PROBLEMS
INTO SUCCESS STORIES

HANDLE RETURNS GRACIOUSLY

When a customer requests a refund, whether cancelling a service or returning a product, **be upbeat, cheerful, and helpful. Tell the customer you're sorry things didn't work out and that you're happy to help.**

Never take a return personally. Your customer may feel awkward about returning the item or cancelling the service, and it's your job to set them at ease.

> It takes 12 positive customer service experiences to make up for one negative one.

Here's How

Smile graciously, show empathy, and say: **"I'm sorry things didn't work out. I'll be happy to assist you."** Then complete the transaction with efficiency, friendliness, and respect.

REMEMBER A return is an opportunity to leave the customer with a positive impression. Handled properly, it leaves the door open for future business.

Customer service is just a day-in, day-out, ongoing, never-ending, unremitting, persevering, and compassionate type of activity.
LEON GORMAN, CEO OF L.L. BEAN

TURN COMPLAINERS INTO ADVOCATES

Think of customer complaints as opportunities. When you handle a complaint promptly and effectively, an unhappy customer can become your best customer — and best word of mouth marketer besides. According to bestselling author Seth Godin, "The best time to do great customer service is when a customer is upset."

Here's How

1. **Let the customer talk and listen attentively.** Sometimes all the customer needs is to vent and have someone listen.

2. **Always say "I'm sorry." Be genuine and mean it.** Never say "Sorry about that" — it doesn't sound sincere.

3. **If the complaint is valid, thank the customer for bringing the problem to your attention.** Assure them that you'll look into it immediately and fix it so it doesn't happen again.

> Satisfied customers who have problems resolved will tell five people about their good experience.

4. **Find the appropriate solution or remedy for your customer.** As you think about a solution, do your best to put yourself in your customer's shoes and provide a solution that would make you happy in their place. Then be sure to ask your customer if they feel the solution is fair.

5. **Follow up with the customer after the problem is corrected.** Thank them again and give them any update

you have on the situation. Make sure they're satisfied with the final outcome.

Create Happy Complainers

My own advice, if you have the authority, is to do what it takes to **make the customer happy the mistake or problem occurred.** You do this by **overcompensating for the mistake** if it truly was your fault. This kind of thing should only happen once in a while, and your goal should be to make the customer eager to do business with you again and to turn them into your best ambassador.

If you don't have the authority to make this type of decision on your own, check with your supervisor to see if there's anything special you can do for the customer. If not, sometimes a sincere apology, an understanding smile, and the assurance that it will never happen again may be enough.

One day I placed a carry out order for a box of roasted chicken. When I arrived to pick it up, the person working the counter told me he was sorry but my order hadn't been fired (sent to the cooks), so it was going to be another 10 minutes.

"I can take 25% off your order and give you some free bread sticks with cheese," he said. "Does that sound okay to you? Again, I'm really sorry." I told him it sounded great and that I'd be in my truck reading. He asked me which vehicle was mine, and I was pleasantly surprised when, 10 minutes later, he walked out the door and personally delivered my breadsticks and chicken, apologizing again.

"Wow, great service!" I found myself thinking. I've been a long-time customer at this restaurant and this experience only raised my opinion of it. I continue to spread the word about their great food and great service.

When written in Chinese, the word "crisis" is composed of two characters. One represents danger, and the other represents opportunity.
JOHN F. KENNEDY

WHEN THE PROBLEM IS BIG

If a customer comes to you with a big problem and you don't feel comfortable giving them a quick answer, **let them know you'll need a little time to resolve their issue.** Say something like:

> **"I'm very sorry about this. I realize it's very important. Could you please give me a few minutes (or a day if appropriate) to look into it and come up with a fair solution?"**

Another very powerful way to disarm a customer with a complaint is to **acknowledge up front that you may be in the wrong:**

> **"I'm very sorry. We may have made a mistake in your case. Could you please tell me the details and I'll find an answer for you?"**

Never feel that you have to provide an answer right away, especially when it's a tricky, expensive, or questionable transaction. Give yourself time to think about the situation, bounce it off others, and consult a supervisor if needed.

If you're in a hurry, and if your company or supervisor allows it, you're usually safe to use your own best judgment and do the right and fair thing. As part of your solution, **always apologize for**

> It costs five to ten times as much to attract a new customer as it does to keep an existing one.

the mistake by saying "I'm sorry." Accept ownership for the problem, and avoid passing blame.

A Note on "Service Departments"

Any service department must know what its first objective is — and it's *not* to provide service to the customer. As my uncle, sales expert and author Gene Balogh, wrote, "Any customer who gets as far as calling or visiting the service department is frustrated. The first objective of the service department is to unfrustrate the frustrated." Always keep this in mind when working with customers who have complaints!

Customers don't expect you to be perfect. They do expect you to fix things when they go wrong.
DONALD PORTER, DIRECTOR OF CUSTOMER SERVICE
QUALITY ASSURANCE FOR BRITISH AIRWAYS

CREATE A CUSTOMER FOR LIFE

GO THE EXTRA MILE!

UNDER PROMISE, OVER DELIVER

Most businesses over promise and under deliver. They promise more than they can deliver and end up disappointing their customers.

You can stand out from the crowd by doing the opposite: *Under* **promise and** *over* **deliver.** This powerful maxim is credited to bestselling business writer Tom Peters. It works, he says, because "people love surprises, especially the good kind."

Here's How

If you work in a doctor's office, don't put your patient in a waiting room and tell them "The doctor will be in to see you in a few minutes" if you know the wait will be 30 minutes or even an hour.

Be up front and explain to the patient that the doctor is busy and that the wait could be up to an hour. Tell them you'd be happy to get them something to read and let them know you'll check in on them after 30 minutes if they haven't been seen yet. That way, they'll be fine if the doctor sees them in an hour, and pleasantly surprised if the doctor arrives early.

When in doubt, err on the side of caution. Give your customer the longest reasonable wait or delivery time (except in situations where doing so might jeopardize a sale). They'll be surprised and delighted if they get more than promised and they won't be disappointed if they don't.

The same applies to almost any other business or service situation. If you know you can deliver a certain number of

pieces by a particular date, promise on the lower side —
then surprise your customer with the extra windfall. Promise the usual and go out of your way to deliver the amazing!

Word of mouth relies on exceeded expectations.
MARTIN LINDSTROM, AUTHOR OF *BUYOLOGY*

WHEN YOU DON'T KNOW THE ANSWER, ASK

When you don't know the answer to a customer's question, **never just say "I don't know" without offering to find the answer.**

Instead, be honest and say: **"That's a great question. I don't know the answer, but I'll find someone who does so they can help you."**

Or, **"I don't know the answer, but I'll find out and get back to you as soon as possible."**

Fifty-eight percent of buyers report that sales representatives are unable to answer their questions effectively.

MAKE IT EASY FOR CUSTOMERS TO BUY FROM YOU

When a customer makes a reasonable request, reply with **"Yes, I'd be happy to do that!"**

Never say "I can't" or "I'm sorry, that's our policy." Instead, **listen to the customer and do your best to help them and fulfill their request.** Assume they wouldn't be asking if the issue wasn't important to them.

> Americans tell an average of 15 people about good customer service experiences.

If you can't help the customer or don't have the authority to address their issue, locate someone who does. If you're unable to do this immediately, take a message and tell them you'll get back to them with an answer.

REMEMBER Going the extra mile is a powerful way to surprise and delight your customers and build loyalty and respect for your business!

Instead of saying no, figure out a way to say yes!
KIRT MANECKE, AUTHOR OF THIS BOOK

PUT THE CUSTOMER FIRST

When a customer calls your business and asks for something you don't do or carry and you're not able to get it for them, **offer genuine suggestions of other products or services, or refer them to another business that has what they need.**

If you have names, numbers, directions, or hours handy, or can look them up, provide them with these, as well. The customer will never forget your superior service.

Remember the story of Macy's and Gimbels from the Christmas movie *Miracle on 34th Street*? In the movie, the real Kris Kringle gets a job as a department store Santa at Macy's. When he tells a mother she can buy better skates for her child at Gimbels, Macy's biggest competitor, the mother is thrilled but Macy's managers are furious — until the media picks up the story about Macy's "Christmas spirit" and Gimbels returns the favor. In the end, business booms for both stores.

This Christmas classic really gets it right — great service drives referrals and extraordinary sales!

When you enchant people, your goal is not to make money from them or to get them to do what you want, but to fill them with great delight.
GUY KAWASAKI, FORMER APPLE EXECUTIVE
AND AUTHOR OF *ENCHANTMENT*

NEXT STEPS

The great thing about customer service and sales is that any of us can make customers smile and sell more by following practical tips and techniques.

To learn more, visit the *Smile* website at:

www.SmiletheBook.com

NOTES

Introduction

1 The deli welcomes over. "Ari Weinzweig," *ZingTrain,*
http://www.zingtrain.com/about-us/ari-weinzweig/ (accessed
June 8, 2012).

1 Boasts sales of more than. Katie Frank, ZingTrain
Consultant, Telephone Interview with Author, June 11, 2012.

2 Sixty-two percent of consumers. "Zendesk Infographic:
Social Media and the Future of Customer Support," *Column
Five,* http://columnfivemedia.com/work-items/zendesk-
infographic-social-media-and-the-future-of-customer-support/
(accessed June 10, 2012).

2 These consumers will typically. "Social Media Raises the
Stakes for Customer Service," *American Express,* May 2, 2012,
http://about.americanexpress.com/news/pr/2012/gcsb.aspx
(accessed June 6, 2012).

2 Will typically tell over 50 potential. "Social Media Raises
Stakes," *American Express.*

2 And overall, one in four consumers. Harris Interactive,
*2011 Customer Experience Impact Report: Getting to the
Heart of the Consumer and Brand Relationship* (RightNow
Technologies, 2012), 3.

3 A satisfied (but formerly frustrated). John Goodman,
TARP Worldwide Vice Chairman, Telephone Communication
with Author, June 27, 2012.

4 While 80% of companies *think*. James Allen, Frederick
F. Reichheld, Barney Hamilton, and Rob Markey, *Closing the
Delivery Gap: How to Achieve True Customer-Led Growth* (Bain
& Company, Inc., 2005), 1.

4 Nine in ten Americans say. "Social Media Raises Stakes,"
American Express.

4 Poor customer service costs. *The Cost of Poor Customer*

Service: The Economic Impact of the Customer Experience in the U.S. (Genesys, October 2009), 4.

Chapter 1: The Top Ten

12 Indifference is one of the biggest. Lisa Earle McLeod, "How to Get Your Employees to Treat Customers Better," *Forbes.com,* April 26, 2010, www.forbes.com/2010/04/26/customer-service-marketing-leadership-managing-communication.html (accessed June 8, 2012).

12 First impressions occur. Malcolm Gladwell, Interview with Allan Gregg, "Allan Gregg: Malcolm Gladwell — Blink — Full Show," *TVO,* November 5, 2010, http://ww3.tvo.org/video/163858/malcolm-gladwell-blink-full-show (accessed July 3, 2012).

12 Martin Lindstrom discusses. Martin Lindstrom, *Buyology: Truth and Lies About Why We Buy* (New York: Broadway Books, 2010), 60, 76.

14 Shoppers who interact more. Paco Underhill, *Why We Buy: The Science of Shopping* (New York: Simon & Schuster, 1999), 37.

15 When your initial encounter. Lydia Ramsey, "Making the Most of First Impressions," *Lydia Ramsey Business Etiquette Expert,* http://mannersthatsell.com/businessimpressions/ (accessed June 1, 2012).

17 Lack of gratitude is. Katya Andresen, "What Your Donors Aren't Telling You," *Katya's Non-Profit Marketing Blog,* June 26, 2011, www.nonprofitmarketingblog.com/comments/what_your_donors_arent_telling_you/ (accessed June 8, 2012).

19 Seventy percent of small business. U.S. Small Business Administration. Cited in "SBA Study Determines Why Customers Leave," *Nation's Building News Online,* http://www.nbnnews.com/NBN/issues/2005-01-10/Business+Management/2.html (accessed June 13, 2012).

22 Only 38% of salespeople. Dean Davison, "Customer and Market Intelligence for Sales Enablement Success," *Forrester. com*, October 24, 2010, http://blogs.forrester.com/dean_davison/10-10-29-customer_market_intelligence_for_sales_enablement_success (accessed June 15, 2012).

22 Ultimate Buying Motive. Nordic Track Resource Development Department, Sales, *NordicTrack Sales Process Study Guide* (Summer 1994), 6.

22 What's in It for Me? (WIIFM). This is a famous business rule and acronym.

24 The best salespeople are more. Steve W. Martin, "Seven Personality Traits of Top Salespeople," *Harvard Business Review Blog Network,* June 27, 2011, http://blogs.hbr.org/cs/2011/06/the_seven_personality_traits_o.html (accessed June 8, 2012).

26 Even in a tough economy. Harris Interactive, *2009 Customer Experience Impact Report* (RightNow Technologies, 2009), 2.

27 They "product dump." I first heard this term from my wonderful manager Candy at the now defunct company BigChalk.com in Ann Arbor, MI.

27 "People don't need to know." Katya Andresen, *Robin Hood Marketing: Stealing Corporate Savvy to Sell Just Causes* (New York: John Wiley & Sons, Inc., Jossey-Bass, 2006), 16.

Chapter 2: Keep Them Smiling

33 Sixty to sixty-five percent. Judee K. Burgoon, David B. Buller, W. Gill Woodall, *Nonverbal Communication: The Unspoken Dialogue* (New York: McGraw-Hill, 1996), 3.

38 Two in three customers have. "What's Wrong with Customer Service?" *ConsumerReports.org,* July 2011, www.consumerreports.org/cro/magazine-archive/2011/july/shopping/customer-service/overview/index.htm (accessed June 8, 2012).

38 Calls wait time… "exited the place." Paco Underhill, *Why We Buy,* 38.

39 "**Fast, Fun, and Friendly.**" From the company website. "Target Culture," http://sites.target.com/site/en/company/page. jsp?contentId=WCMP04-031452 (accessed June 1, 2012).

42 **In the past year, one in two customers.** "Social Media Raises Stakes," *American Express.*

43 **Sixty percent of millionaires.** *Attracting and Retaining Millionaire Investors* (Spectrem Group, 2010), 17.

45 **Seventy percent of customers.** "Good Service Is Good Business: American Consumers Willing to Spend More with Companies That Get Service Right, According to American Express Survey," *American Express,* May 3, 2011, http://about. americanexpress.com/news/pr/2011/csbar.aspx (accessed June 8, 2012).

45 "**A customer is the most important.**" There is some controversy surrounding the source of this quote, but it is frequently attributed to Mahatma Gandhi.

Chapter 3: Sell More
50 **Consumers cite knowledgeable staff.** *The New Realities of "Dating" in the Digital Age: Are Customers Really Cheating, or Are You Just Not Paying Enough Attention?* (Accenture, 2012), 7.

52 **The idea is to make them more anxious.** My late uncle Gene Balogh taught me this. He was an expert salesman and a very successful trainer and professional speaker specializing in construction industry sales.

56 **Features Tell, Benefits Sell.** This is a famous sales maxim.

63 **In 85% of interactions with prospects.** Richard Fenton. Cited in Bob Janet, "Stop Giving It Away! Don't Be Afraid to Get Paid for Your Services," *EvanCarmichael.com,* http://www. evancarmichael.com/Sales/3081/Stop-Giving-It-Away----Dont-be-afraid-to-get-paid-for-your-services.html (accessed July 24, 2012).

63 Helping the customer buy what they need. I credit my late uncle Gene Balogh for teaching me to think of sales in this way. He taught me to focus on the customer's needs instead of my own and to set my fear aside.

65 "Why did you give?" This is a famous fundraising saying.

68 Suggestive selling can increase. Statistic refers to use of digital signage for suggestive selling. U.S. Small Business Administration. Cited in Elad Halperin, "Top Ten Tips for QSR Suggestive Selling," *QSRweb.com*, March 18, 2010, http://www. qsrweb.com/article/95874/Top-10-tips-for-QSR-suggestive-selling (accessed June 8, 2012).

68 When a customer purchases your product. For more information on suggestive selling and the McDonald's tactic, see Theresa Howard, "'Do You Want Fries with That?': Workers Pushing Extra Sales," *USATODAY.com*, April 10, 2009, www. usatoday.com/money/economy/2009-04-09-upsell-extra-sales_N.htm (accessed June 8, 2012).

71 Only one in six sales professionals. Cited in Todd Kasper, "Key Takeaways from the Chicago Sales 2.0 Conference," *Precallpro.com*, September 17, 2009, http:// www.precallpro.com/blog/bid/20364/Key-Takeways-from-the-Chicago-Sales-2-0-Conference (accessed June 8, 2012).

71 According to the Six P's. This is a popular training and education adage.

72 "Luck is preparation meeting." A similar version of this quote, "Luck is what happens when preparation meets opportunity" is sometimes attributed to Seneca, the Roman philosopher and statesman.

73 The curse of knowledge. This concept originates with Colin Camerer, George Loewenstein, and Martin Weber in "The Curse of Knowledge in Economic Settings: An Experimental Analysis," *Journal of Political Economy* 97, no. 5 (October 1989): 1232-54.

73 Use the word "like." I learned this very useful technique from Chip and Dan Heath in the wonderful book *Made to Stick: Why Some Ideas Survive and Others Die* (New York: Random House, 2007), 57.

Chapter 4: When There's a Problem
76 It takes 12 positive customer service. Cited in "Customer Service Facts,"*CustomerServiceManager.com*, http://www.customerservicemanager.com/customer-service-facts.htm (accessed June 9, 2012).

77 Satisfied customers who have. John Goodman, TARP Worldwide Vice Chairman, Telephone Communication with Author, June 27, 2012.

77 "The best time to do great." Seth Godin, "Winning on the Uphills," *Seth Godin's Blog,* July 21, 2009, http://sethgodin.typepad.com/seths_blog/2009/07/winning-on-the-uphills.html (accessed June 9, 2012).

80 It costs five to ten times. Donna Fenn, "10 Ways to Get More Sales from Existing Customers," *Inc.com,* August 31, 2010, www.inc.com/guides/2010/08/get-more-sales-from-existing-customers.html (June 9, 2012).

81 "Any customer who gets as far as." Quote from my late uncle Gene (Eugene William Balogh), author of *Profitable Construction Sales* (Bloomfield Hills, MI: The Management Center, 1978), during a conversation in June of 2011.

Chapter 5: Create a Customer for Life
84 Under Promise, Over Deliver. This powerful maxim is credited to one of my favorite customer service experts, bestselling business writer Tom Peters. Visit his website at www.tompeters.com.

86 Fifty-eight percent of buyers report. Cited in *A New Vision of Sales Effectiveness: Empowering Sales and Marketing to Succeed in the World of the Buying Cycle* (OutStart, Inc., 2010), 4.

87 Americans tell an average of 15. "Social Media Raises Stakes," *American Express.*

87 Instead of saying no. This is my own advice. I've found that it delights customers and makes my job easier and more rewarding and fulfilling, too!

88 Remember the story of Macy's and Gimbels. To learn more about the movie, visit www.imdb.com/title/tt0039628/.

INDEX

ABOUT THE AUTHOR

Kirt Manecke is a sales, marketing, fundraising, and business development specialist with over 30 years of experience making customers smile. A proven "natural" salesman, Kirt helps companies build lasting, profitable relationships with clients through strategic marketing and expert customer service.

As founder and former owner of an award-winning specialty retail business in Michigan, Kirt created and implemented an innovative six-week training program that maximized customer satisfaction and sales by teaching employees many of the skills presented in *Smile*.

Kirt is currently working on two more books. The first is an advanced version of *Smile* to help individuals maximize sales. The second is a how-to manual for retail business owners to help them design and maintain a winning sales environment.

In his free time, Kirt volunteers his skills to help end animal cruelty and preserve natural areas in the United States and abroad. Kirt is founder and chair of the Michigan chapter of Animals Asia, a group devoted to rescuing animals from cruelty, raising awareness, and improving public policy affecting animals. Learn more about Kirt at www.SmiletheBook.com.